The Grass Dance

by

Laurel Johnson

AmErica House
Baltimore

First printing

ISBN: 1-58851-445-5
PUBLISHED BY AMERICA HOUSE BOOK PUBLISHERS
www.publishamerica.com
Baltimore

Printed in the United States of America

Dedication

I have so many wonderful friends and family,
that it is not possible to mention them all
on one dedication page.
Their support and belief in me has been a godsend.
They know who they are, and that I love and treasure them.
This first book is dedicated to them,
and to Di-angel,
who wanted so much to live to see my books published.
I know she's always somewhere near me in spirit,
rooting me on.

Acknowledgments

Special recognition goes to my Mother,
Grandma and Grandpa Ford,
and their old friend John.
Without them, there would be no story.
I must also mention my husband,
because he lived it with me and stood beside me
through it all.

Introduction

Can you fathom the mysteries of God?
Can you probe the limits of the Almighty?
They are higher than the heavens—what can YOU do?
They are deeper than the depths of the grave—what can YOU know?
Their measure is longer than the earth
and wider than the sea.

–Job Chapter 11: verses 7-9

Part One

The Broken Circle

God's continuum begins
before we're formed inside our mother's womb,
so says the ancient psalmist,
and continues far beyond the grave.
Our lives become one endless vital circle,
encompassing the ancestors who lived before us
back through time
and those who follow after in the future.
Who mends our circle when it breaks?
God alone can make it whole again.

Chapter One

The Grave

My pilgrimage began as it would eventually end, in the Potawotomi County cemetery. At the foot of a grave, staring at its crumbling sandstone marker, is not the place I would have chosen for an epiphany. Still, that place had special meaning for me.

At one time, the gravestone had a name carved into it—Indian John. Every summer of my life my grandparents had visited this obscure place in the rolling Kansas prairies to decorate John's grave. From earliest childhood, I can recall my Grandma whispering solemnly while sorting through her hand picked flowers, "And we MUST fix something nice for John." No Decoration Day went by without visiting John's grave.

John had no other name I was aware of, no history except for what he'd shared with Grandma and Grandpa. But it was clear from the way she spoke his name that John was someone of importance to them both.

In the years when they were younger and more flexible, the three of us would sit beside John's grave while Grandma and Grandpa relived old memories of their days on the farm. We'd lounge upon the grass and I would listen raptly as they talked. With the coming of adulthood nothing changed, except my grandma grew progressively more feeble and the trips to visit Indian John at rest became more difficult for them to navigate. Grandpa and I would have to hold Grandma up by both arms while I clutched the bouquet for John tightly in my free hand. Their ritual never varied much, once we finally reached his grave.

Grandma would say, “Here lies the best friend we ever had.” She would try, not too successfully, to hold back tears each time she said it. “He worked for Dad’s folks, you know.”

Dad referred to my grandpa, who stood by in silence smiling, nodding, choked up with emotion. These two blessed and beloved anchors of my life would weep in silence for awhile each year in honor of a long dead friend, their mysterious John.

Tenderly and reverently, the flowers Grandma’s gnarled arthritic hands had gathered would be placed upon the grave, next to the headstone. She would smile and softly sniff a laugh like people sometimes do when they’ve been crying, and her eyes would meet with Grandpa’s. He would smile that twinkling-eyed smile of his and nod at her as if they shared some special and unspoken secret. That would be my cue to ask the question I’d been asking them for decades: “How did you and John become such good friends?”

My grandparents took great delight in the telling of their story, and I had never tired of hearing it. I’d never met their friend, this man who died back in the early 1920s, and yet their memories of John made him seem to be alive and standing with us.

John was ancient when they met him, wrinkled bronze and wiry from a life of heavy labor and sparse living. All they knew of him at first was that he grew his own tobacco in a shed half tumbled down from Kansas winds and weather, and he lived in that same shed of his own choosing.

John worked for Grandpa's parents on the farm. He stayed to himself, kept his own thoughts, and rarely spoke a word aloud, but he took an instant liking to my grandpa. Grandpa was a big hard working man of strong Germanic stock, who smiled a lot and loved to pull an often not-so-gentle prank.

John accepted Grandpa's joking without comment, and he loved my grandma's doughnuts with an almost childlike fervor.

"John would have worked for doughnuts if we'd let him," Grandma often said, while Grandpa nodded his agreement with that statement. In all his days, no one had ever made John doughnuts and delivered them to his shed with morning coffee. No one else had ever fried a fluffy doughnut and coated it so proudly with sugar for no other reason than to brighten John's morning. No one else in THOSE parts had ever looked beyond John's "hired man" status and taken him into their circle of life.

Except for gladly eating Grandma's doughnuts and drinking the coffee she laced with heavy cream and sugar the way he liked it, John avoided them at first. Inevitably though, as time passed, John's life became entwined with theirs.

Silently and stoically he loved their babies just as he loved Grandma and Grandpa. He tended to their fevers, eased their pains with plants and herbs he gathered, making pastes and salves and poultices and harsh foul tasting teas to treat each illness. Grandma paid him off in doughnuts and with home-cooked meals he shared at table on the rare occasion he agreed to that luxury.

John became their guardian, protector, hunkered down

outside their door with murmured prayer songs in the night when they were sick or troubled. A pile of weathered oak would show up just outside their door in winter, or an offering of fresh caught fish or quail would come at just the time they needed it the most. He knew their hearts and they knew his like no one ever has, before or since.

John wouldn't go to "white man's church" when Grandpa asked him to attend and sit with him and Grandma. He said, "No!" and poked one index finger towards the heavens saying, "I know God." In every way a mortal could, John demonstrated that he did, indeed, know God. He lived his life as honestly and truthfully as he knew how. He practiced patience and kindness every day with everyone he came across. His face just fairly glowed with God's goodness, Grandma said, and yet John had never gone to church or read a Bible because he couldn't read. Grandma gave him a small Bible anyway because she thought that having it might make John proud and happy.

He kept the Bible wrapped inside a square of cloth resurrected from the confines of his shed.

Grandpa said John used to set a bit of time aside each day while it was light to look at pages in the Bible. He said that John believed the black marks in his book were words that God had written personally for him. John called looking at the black marks "studying his lessons," and struggled every day to gain a bit of wisdom from them.

Sometimes while studying, John said, "I see..." as if a bit of truth had been revealed to him. Other times he'd say, "Oh pshaw..." in mimicry of Grandpa.

They watched his struggles from a distance, and found

John's innocence to be endearing.

The winter their friend died, he came to them all smiles one crisp clear Kansas morning. Grandma always said that she could still see John's breath with every word he spoke to them that day. Decades had passed since John's death, but she could call up his last words from fading memories as if they had been spoken only hours before. John seldom smiled, and so it was an unaccustomed happy look he gave them on his final day of living on this earth.

"I wish you both long life and many years together." He clenched a work worn hand and laid it soft against his chest that morning. "We made one living circle of our lives. I take you with me as I go to my Creator."

For John to speak in such a way surprised them and they didn't fully understand his meaning at that moment. "Please don't forget me Herb and Esther."

It was the first time John had ever used their given names. Oh how that pleased them coming from a man like John! I can't explain their happiness at hearing John speak their names, except perhaps that those were times when people spoke with less familiarity than they do now. Perhaps it had to do with John accepting at the end of his life that he was more than a hired hand to them. Or maybe it was because he finally understood that they considered him their friend and equal and always had. They both vowed solemnly to John that they would not forget him, not ever, then watched as their friend walked slowly towards his shed.

Grandpa found him later, "gone to rest" as Grandma called it. She said it just about grieved them both half to death when they lost John. The only thing that eased their sadness, Grandma said, was knowing that John went to live in heaven with the God he wanted so much to understand.

They found a place for John to rest amongst their dead friends and relatives, and managed to afford that one small gravestone. They chose a lovely quiet spot where John could have eternal sleep with peace.

After much discussion, it was decided they should mark it with the name he'd always gone by, Indian John. To them, however, he always and forever would be, simply, their friend, John.

Somehow I always felt like John was my friend, too. Although he died more than twenty years before I was born, I felt connected to him. John was real to me just like my grandparents were, a part of the continuum connecting present, past, and future times together in life's circle.

Despite the many twists and turns my life has taken, I have been proven right to think of John that way.

Chapter Two

Lessons Forgotten

I said the story began in the cemetery at the foot of Indian John's grave and so it did. Many of life's simple truths were learned there, but as years passed and my grandparents aged, we finally stopped our annual ritual at his grave.

This time began the darkest period of my life. My struggles would eventually lead to regained peace and contentment, but I had no way of knowing that at the time my trials began.

For reasons I will never fully understand, a part of me began to forget the lessons I had learned over the years from Grandma, Grandpa, and Mom. I forgot for a time the truths I'd learned in Sunday School and church, forgot a loving God created everything, forgot the Baby Jesus and His legacy of love. My world, that once had made such sense and seemed so simple, gradually lost focus. For lack of a better word, I disconnected from the people and beliefs that had given my life meaning. I felt alone and abandoned, living in a broken circle of confusion that would last for many years and not be mended any time soon. This is my story, told in prose and verse because that is the only way I know to share it, told so I will never again forget the lessons I learned from Grandma, Grandpa, Mom and John.

I began to lose myself not too long after the last trip we took together to the cemetery. The first time I had to go alone—Grandma would not hush til I did—I took one look at that long straight white gravel road that led past the cemetery and went into a panic. I had been feeling unequal to any task, inept and insecure, lost. Even a simple thing like decorating our old friend John's grave seemed too difficult for me that day.

My mind was full of death and worldly cynicism. Grandpa had unexpectedly died as he lived, without fanfare. I'd never see those twinkling blue eyes again. My Grandpa had died, and with him all the memories we shared, or so I thought at the time. I hummed a tuneless death song while searching for John's grave.

Where was it? I lashed, out cursing at the thought of paying tribute to the man without his two dear friends and mine completing one full circle at his grave. I wept and raged until I almost went insane to think that I had lost John's grave, lost my grandpa, and was slowly losing myself.

The death song I'd been humming took on words. I sat down among the grass and wildflowers growing all around me, and I cried. Something shuddered. I didn't know if that one trembling movement was the earth or me because my world was out of kilter at that moment.

That day I did something that was not customary for me. I gave in to defeat and despair. I didn't think about how wonderful it was that Grandpa was in heaven, no longer old and sick. I didn't use my time that quiet summer afternoon to think back fondly on all the lessons Grandpa taught me by example or of the happy years we'd been together. I didn't spend that time alone giving thanks for having such a Grandpa in my life. Instead, I raged because I'd lost him and my mind created death songs that revisited the day he died. His death and how his sweet familiar face looked that day still haunted me back then.

Death Song

A friend looked out at me through empty eyes today,
and now the jokes and smiles and easy talks are gone.
No more exchange of information or emotion.
No laughter, tears, no secrets from our youth,
for half of everything we talked about is lost.
My God, the shock of it!
To see that empty face devoid of life!
I knew him well, and now,
no more my friend, he lies before me lifeless.
And Death has not the grace to close his eyes.

I lied when I got back to Grandma's, pretended I had found John's grave quite easily and put her flowers on it. I lied so she would not be disappointed in me. I lied as I had never lied before, for any reason. And later on at home my husband knew that I was slipping and he could not stop it.

I was restless, lost in thought, and sleep would not come. I had always "slept the sleep of the angels," as I called it, peacefully and restfully, but now sleep would not come at all. I lied when he asked me if something was wrong. I lied so he would not worry. I lied. And with every lie I forgot more of the lessons I had learned in better times. I began to think that I heard weeping in the night, silent soulful weeping. Those night cries were a warning of more bad times to come, but I did not heed them.

I took to having wild imaginings at night. I traced the shadows on the wall with fevered fingertips. I laid down and sought the coldness of the floor against my cheek and imagined that my aura slipped away while blind with lunar light.

Night after night I searched for answers in my soul and prayed to find a welcoming in places yet unknown. From past experience I knew that peaceful place of welcoming existed in God's presence, but I was lost and could not find my way there. Instead I heard crying in the night and hoped for reassurance that the weeping was not mine.

My husband would have helped me if he could have. All he knew was that the once bright, loving woman that he married had been slowly disappearing over time. He blamed himself in silence, cried in secret, certain it was something he had done or not done that had driven me inside myself.

In my mind I was clinging to him like a half-mad thing in my attempts to keep from drowning. He thought of me as silent, sullen, and withdrawn. I wrote poems hoping to express what I was feeling because I couldn't seem to say it any other way. He couldn't grasp my obtuse way of speaking, couldn't understand my silent misery. Many sadnesses would pass between us before either of us fully understood.

I gave my husband poems thinking they were tributes. He often cried because he knew me well enough to know my poems represented loss, but had no idea loss of what. My mind was in a shambles, but I knew he loved me. Often knowing that was all that got me through my day intact and breathing. I felt drained dry, laying in a wasted place of broken dreams and shattered circles I could not hang onto anymore. He saw life in simpler terms, with hope. He provided the one remaining anchor I required to keep my balance, but he could not help me. He watched numbly from the sidelines as I gave myself over to other worldly means of making sense of my existence. He watched me as I turned away from God.

It was difficult for him to accept. For years I'd been predictable, had followed the same path. I'd participated in church and community activities, kept a calm and uncluttered home. I'd read my Bible daily and reassured him when his spirits flagged. All of that changed overnight, without a warning.

I put my Holy Bibles on the shelf and in their place came weirdness, casting lots, all manner of occult experiments that frightened him beyond expression. I started with the "I Ching," and when that did not provide the answers to my seeking I progressed to the "Mandala" and other occult practices I can't remember now. I had no idea what they represented, and ignored the fact that the occult was labeled an abomination by God. Divined messages of death and dark fates were all the spirits gave me. My desperation and anxiety grew in direct proportion to how often I attempted to divine my future using occult means.

My husband burned the hateful books of divination; I bought more. He tried to enlist the help of my friends by telling them how lost I was. They laughed and said, "If SHE is crazy, all of us are close behind." They can't be blamed for their response because I hid my madness well from everyone.

Only my husband could see it. He suffered in his isolation and held on to me as best he could. He read my poetry in secret as he prayed to God for guidance through the maze our life together had become. He waited, watched and worried, prayed for a solution that would be a long time coming.

Chapter Three

Beyond Burnout

The creeping madness eventually spilled over into my work world. I couldn't hide it any longer. First came illnesses both real and psychological. Puzzled doctors who were also co-workers or friends could not diagnose my illness.

Doctors often are bewildered by the spiritual illnesses they see, and so they failed to find a lasting cure. First they had me take time off from work, then cut back on work hours and extra-curricular activities. They did CAT scans, x-rays, blood tests. They tried hospitalizations and medications. Nothing helped.

Finally, they pronounced me tired but well, stressed but not beyond endurance.

Left to my own devices, I began to put my weirdness onto paper, written words that drove me deeper into madness and despair. I projected that despair into my marriage, into friendships that were strained beyond endurance by my bizarre and uncharacteristic behavior. I tried to smile and act like my normal self with Mother and Grandma because I feared that they would see in me the shadow person I was rapidly becoming. If they noticed a difference in me, neither of them mentioned it.

My friends and poor beleaguered husband thought that I no longer loved them. I stopped reaching out in kindness and compassion in my total self-absorption. The doctors called it burnout.

At the time, I tried to put a positive spin on my disintegrating life. I accepted the burnout diagnosis and tried to understand what had thrown me into it. I asked myself what breaks people down into tiny fragments of their former selves, into shards and shiny bits that never seem to fit together once the whole is broken. I wondered what leaves people half insane with grief and loss amidst the tattered remnants of their lives. I thought maybe I had seen too much illness and trauma and had become too personally involved with the sadness. Had I lived within a framework of ideals that were impossible to reach? Had my once empathetic leanings far outstripped my strength? What hope was left for me if I had broken in the pursuit of youthful dreams that fizzled or flamed out when faced with harsh reality? There was no simple explanation. All I saw was the results. I had gone beyond burnout. Nothing but the grace of God could bring me back to fight another day.

I do realize now that in my case it wasn't burnout. Oh, for many years I told myself it was because burnout was an easy explanation. I still worked a full time job when I was able and made excuses for myself when I was lacking. I still attended church and went through all the motions, but I didn't read my Bible anymore or talk to God the way I used to. The name "Jesus" did not cross my lips except to blaspheme. I'd forgotten all about the graveyard and the lessons I had learned there. I'd forgotten all about respect and friendship and the circle that connects us to each other, and our God.

Every life is full of testing, laced with sorrows we must share with one another and our families. Every life encounters hardships that we muddle through somehow if we remember where our comfort comes from when we need it.

I don't know what made me lose my focus on the lessons I had learned. I don't know what made me lose all hope or trust in family and God. All I can tell you for certain as I look back on all that happened is that somehow evil gained a foothold in my life. I didn't deliberately seek evil or consciously acknowledge its existence, but evil took me over for a time. It wasn't a dramatic evil like we see in movies or read about in novels. I did not become a vile monster who set out to harm those around me. Subtle changes simply overtook my thinking and my life began to unravel.

How could this have happened to me? My life had been built on the firm foundation of family, God's truths, and love. I considered myself to be stable, reasonably intelligent, and mature. How, in one fell swoop, had my life gone so out of balance?

Grandma used to say when people turned away from God and reaped a bitter harvest in return that they were "fallen." That was her catch-all term for lives that had taken a negative turn, for whatever reason. Whenever ugliness moved in and crowded out the good, or people allowed dark thoughts to be more powerful than happy ones, my Grandma called it "fallen."

She used to say "I've fallen once or twice myself and it's no fun," meaning, she felt hopeless or depressed or angry, gone beyond the loving reach of God in her despair. Or she would shake her head and say that someone had fallen and we all needed to pray for them. I must confess it never made much sense to me until I was the "fallen" one!

Grandma's ways were wiser ways than mine by far, so I

defer to her in this.

My conclusion looking back in retrospect is that I was fallen, not burned out. I was fallen, not suffering with clinical depression or exhaustion. I was fallen and had turned my back on God because, for whatever reason, His goodness was forgotten by me for awhile.

Chapter Four

Mother

Somehow I reached a state of being quietly unbalanced for awhile. I used "I Ching" and horoscopes to run my daily life, fancied myself to be a "white witch" of the highest order like Grandma's father had been. I'd heard Grandma's stories of white witchcraft so often in the past, how her father said it was a power passed from father to daughter, daughter to son, down through the generations. She said it was a thing to fear, not envy or acquire. She said that only God and His Word gave us the answers we should live by.

All my life I had believed what Grandma and the Bible said about occult practices, until suddenly, I became a walking testament to other worldly powers not of God. I abandoned God and all His teachings because in my misery, I thought He had abandoned me.

Eventually there has to come a time when madness ends, or culminates in changes. I had reached what I considered a "position" in my work. (This was, of course, due to my self appointed powers as a seeress, or so I told myself.) I had worked on my behavior til it reached the point of not being outright weird at least. The illnesses I'd been suffering no longer troubled me. I was convinced the worst was over, when in truth it was just beginning.

Thus far I've not discussed my mother. I adored her in the

same way I did her parents, with devotion and a softness that not even my madness could destroy. Mom had been a pretty woman all her life. In her younger years she was coquettish, with a flair for wearing just the right amount of makeup to accentuate her skin and hair. Mom would have been quite stylish, if only she could have afforded a more extensive wardrobe. All through high school she had eyes only for the man who would become my father. They made a striking couple in their youth when life was good for them and full of hope.

Mom was pretty on the inside, also, where a woman ought to be, despite the disappointments in her life. I admired her for the courage and sweet nature that somehow survived her marriage to my alcoholic father who beat her and their children. She despised the almost-poverty their divorce had thrown us into but she had no grand illusions about knights in shining armor or some unexpected windfall. She did her best to raise four children within her limited financial abilities. Mom fed and clothed us, kept a roof over our heads, and raised us on the teachings of a loving Jesus. I learned lessons from my mother like the ones I learned from Grandma and Grandpa—love of family and God and fellow man, respect and kindness, simple faith, being thankful, and forgiveness. On the outside, Mom seemed soft and vulnerable, easily wounded, but in the heart of her she was unswerving in her strength and determination. Above all other humans, I admired her.

It was a cold November day when Mom called me on the phone and said she had something to show me. The second I saw her face I braced myself. It was a look of quiet horror on her face, a look of desperate hope that something I might say would save her. She said "I have a doctor's appointment today, will you go with me?" I can still feel the warmth of her hand as she took hold of mine and laid it softly on the underside of her breast. I can still feel the way my mind went cold the second my hand cupped the red and draining orange-sized mass. I can still feel the ache of my face contorting into anguish and the muscles of my throat contracting with rage. I can still feel the burning in my belly and the way my tears felt pouring out when I said, "Mom..."

I couldn't save her and she knew it in that moment, as did I. We suffered miserably together through that day and all the ones that followed. Oh, we made the most of it and put on our brave fronts. We pretended that the doctor was quite right in saying that it might not be as bad as it looked.

We made a big production of decorating her hospital room for Christmas. We took great pains to make it seem far less horrific than it was so no one would believe her days were numbered. We went through the surgery and planned the radiation treatments and chemotherapy with pretend hope, feigned faith. She spoke of prayer and thought that God might heal her. I squared my shoulders and stubbornly pressed on without Him.

For a time, all thoughts of casting lots and the occult were gone. All thoughts and energies were poured into my mother and her needs. I began to think if only I tried hard enough, put enough personal energy into her, that my beliefs and strengths alone would be enough to save her.

Round after dreadful round of cobalt was soon followed by chemotherapy. Months went by, and then a couple years. The chemicals and radiation took a mighty toll on Mom, but she improved awhile with every round.

Eventually, her appetite began to fail. I knew that was a fearsome sign. Our family on my mother's side had always been big eaters no matter what befell us. No one ever lost their appetite. It was October 1984, and that year fall meant nothing to me, although in better times, it was my favorite season. I hadn't written poetry in quite some time because all feeling and emotion died the day I saw the lump on Mother's breast.

But one crisp sunny morning in the first week of October I sat down to put what I was feeling onto paper. God had been on my mind that day. It was not the God of my youth, nor the God I had shared with my Grandma and Grandpa and Mom that came to mind. It was a God that I perceived as vengeful, a cruel God I thought about. The poem came easily to me. I see it now as quite symbolic that I folded up the finished poem and placed it in the center of my Living Bible that had been upon a shelf unread for several years.

I Am Not God

I've never quite recovered
or forgiven God for letting you be taken
from the life you planned into this nightmare
of harsh medicines and cobalt.
Of all the souls in all the world
who might have benefited from the lessons
that a slow and painful death can teach
you were the LAST one I would have chosen.
But then, I am not God now, am I.
If I were God, you would have had
a life of blessed peace and fun,
a husband who adored you, and
the money to do anything you pleased.
If I were God, no one would dare
to say or think—as many did—
when you were young and married Dad,
"She made her bed, she was a fool,
now let her lie in it, poor thing."
But then, I am not God now, am I.
If I were God, the cruel among us
would be tortured, burned with cobalt,
stripped to the bone with chemotherapy,
and robbed of all their hopes and dreams.
I can't continue with this tirade.
God knows how I feel if he is real.
He'll take you from me anyway
and I will have to swallow down my rage.
It wouldn't be this way if I were God.

My heart was pounding as I put that poem in between the pages of what used to be my favorite Bible. My head felt hot and four times its normal size, as if it might explode.

I tried to shake a feeling of disaster; like I'd reached a place where going back or even forward was no longer possible. I can still see the sun shining on the kitchen carpet as I headed for the basement. Clothes I'd washed and dried for Mom were waiting to be folded. I picked up a duster she had worn the day before to chemotherapy. From that point on, for many months, I would remember only fragments of my life and little else.

That day, a man I did not recognize, wearing a fishing hat that looked familiar as I recall, was bending over me and asking me what happened. A dog whose name I did not know was licking me as I sat on the basement floor. All I can remember saying to the man and the dog is, "I'm rattled," as if they could explain that feeling to me.

The stranger in a fishing hat led me upstairs into a house I did not recognize and sat me on an unfamiliar couch. He used the phone to make a call and whispered to that someone on the other end that I had fallen down or something and I wasn't acting right. The stranger acted nervous and kept looking at me as if I ought to know him. He asked me questions I could not comprehend, although I struggled to find answers that would please him until I started crying with the strain of it.

Friends came and went. I knew only one of them and called that friend by name—Sam—but could not quite remember how I knew her. I studied the faces of each new person I saw, hoping for a spark of recognition I could build on. Most of them realized with a sick suddenness that I did not remember who they were. I chose to use that particular term—sick suddenness—because of the sick looks that suddenly came over their faces when I stared back at them blankly.

A doctor came and made himself at home as if he knew me well, but he was just another stranger. He smiled a lot and kept assuring everyone that I was fine and that whatever had happened to me would be temporary.

I did not remember my husband or friends, my work. I could not recall that my mother lived one block down the street from me or that her days were numbered. I'd forgotten my grandma and grandpa, the happy days of childhood, the trips to John's grave before the circle of our lives was broken.

The names of my sisters and brother, or even that they existed, had been lost to me. Gone also was any thought of the "I Ching," white witchcraft, or the occult practices that had so completely wrecked my world. I'd forgotten everything, both good and bad. My mind was empty, waiting to be filled again.

My mind was empty, but at last that awful rage was gone.

Chapter Five

Voices

I'm not sure if that sudden onset of amnesia was an ending or a beginning.

My mother blamed herself, of course, which made the last few weeks of her life sadder. My husband blamed himself, and was even more bewildered by this sudden loss of memories than he had been by my years of strange behavior.

My boss was certain that my job responsibilities had escalated beyond my ability to cope. He said my loss of memory must be job related. I couldn't reassure them because I didn't know, could not recall a thing from early childhood on.

Mother died that same year. One late night she simply went to sleep, with peace. I didn't treasure the sweet smile that formed the minute of her passing, or comprehend the gentle "Nitey nite" she spoke before she died.

It didn't hit me like it should have at the time because I had forgotten everything she did for me and meant to me. I had forgotten her quiet love of God and her belief that heaven was a brighter, happier place than earth had ever been. I went to her funeral in a state of confusion, not grieving or recalling what I'd lost. I did not believe she was with God and refused to listen to anyone who said she was.

In the months that followed Mother's death, I worked at

regaining lost memories and abilities. I couldn't resume my work as a Registered Nurse because I couldn't remember skills I'd learned in school or in the twenty years of my profession. I worked as a nurse's aide at first and followed directions rather woodenly, I thought. Strangely, I had not forgotten how to type, so I typed medical transcription in the afternoons. This, of course, was on the days I didn't go to the psychiatrist who charged a whopping fee to sleep while I was talking. He scoffed at any thoughts I had of God and my belief that if only I could reconcile myself with God somehow, my situation would improve.

Over eight months time my memories returned by fits and starts. I did relearn much of what I'd known, like cooking, making coffee. My nursing skills and memories returned quite rapidly it seemed to me, while other thoughts, of childhood for example, came back incomplete or in fragments.

My husband thought a new start was in order, and I agreed quite willingly. I wanted to see hope in his face again, to somehow lessen his burden of worry over me. If he thought moving was the answer, I was for it.

We moved across the country, far from home, to my husband's native state, Kentucky. I coldly turned my back and left behind my family and friends. I drove away and left my grandma sitting, crying on her porch, without one conscious thought of all the times we'd shared there. I gladly moved away in search of something undefined, thinking all my troubles would be left behind. They weren't.

My recounting of this story seems superficial for good reason. I can't remember many details of those years or the ones preceding. It's like another person lived it and forgot to tell me everything. What fragments I relate have been snatched back from the brink of almost gone. I do remember that more than just my husband and our dogs arrived there to live in the Kentucky Appalachians. Invisible apparitions came along for the ride.

We had many old and dear friends in Kentucky, as we did in Kansas. Many wonderful people lived there who had known my husband all his life. But even our new start amongst the glorious Kentucky highlands would be flawed by my condition.

We could not make a go of our life there because of me.

While driving through deep forests on curving mountain roads I actively hallucinated. Imaginary people told me where to go and what to do. Perhaps nobody noticed, but I lost touch with all reality and struggled to maintain a half-sane balance.

There were mundane activities like dealing with my co-workers and the patients I saw as a home health nurse. There were decisions to be made, such as where to plant our rose bushes and trees. And there was sitting in the porch swing watching it rain. I made out checks and paid the bills on time the way I always had. Every seemingly normal activity was overshadowed by my fear that the imaginary people would become my reality.

These people, quite invisible to everyone but me, were with me every minute of the day and often in the night. One was a solemn child who begged for me to stop and play awhile. The second was a grim-faced nun who chanted prayers from dawn til midnight every day without ceasing. The last and strongest was a foul-mouthed, wild-haired woman who encouraged me to break the law and lose my cautious nature for a while. Their chatter was a constant source of aggravation and confusion while I struggled to maintain my daily life. I called my Kansas headshrinker out of desperation and asked him what they meant. He said they meant my personality had shattered and to find a doctor in Kentucky who could give me medication. Medication wasn't what I needed, and I know that now in retrospect.

Something in me just kept holding onto hope that someday I would be myself again. I hung onto constants in my life like Grandma and my sisters, my brother, friends in Kansas and Kentucky, and my husband. I called Grandma every Sunday from Kentucky, and listened while she talked of "Dad" and all the other joys and sorrows she recalled from over eighty years of living. I could still connect with Grandma, understand what she was saying, and feel almost whole each time I heard her voice.

We lasted only eighteen months in our new life before we knew it was a failed escape. Actually, I guess we might have stayed there in Kentucky, but one day I wandered off and headed west accompanied by my three persistent non-existent friends. I have no memory of my trip across the country except I thought that they were driving while I slept. I "woke up" as we were crossing the Missouri River, several hundred miles from home. No message had been left to ease my husband's worry. I simply left Kentucky without warning, heading west.

Yes, my husband followed. His fury and exasperation with my antics knew no bounds I'm sure, and yet he followed and we bought another home in Kansas. I was back to the familiar, back with Grandma once again. It eased me for a time to know I could be with her. Oh, but what a lot of precious time I'd wasted! Years of good times with my Mom and Grandma had been thrown away because Laurel didn't heed the lessons they'd been teaching by example.

I spent as much time as I could with Grandma, but she was different, thinner, weaker, and more fragile with each passing day. She fell a lot, forgot that Grandpa had been dead for years. Her slow slide into dementia was unstoppable, made all the sadder by her knowing that her mind was slipping. She had always been so capable and tough, strong of will and mind, curious and humorous and bright. The woman who had been a stalwart constant in my life was nearly gone, replaced by a helpless childish person who often did not know me.

My sister Pam and I took turns checking on Grandma in the night, in secret. Her madness raged all night inside the house as we rocked in the porch swing, listening and watching. She sometimes worked through the night hours, until she was exhausted, preparing non-existent meals for farmhands on the "home place." Other times she talked all night to her favorite brother, Al, who had been dead for fifty years or more.

By day she would often erupt in violent rages, lashing out with canes or plates of food—whatever she could lay her hands on—to protect herself from loved ones she no longer recognized. I'd have done just about anything for Grandma, but I couldn't keep her living safely in her home or bring her mind back. She would soon be heading for the nursing home, a thing she'd always feared far worse than dying.

I began composing a poem for her, sitting on her porch at midnight in the summer, while she ranted in her bedroom. A warm breeze stirred her favorite wind chimes while she offered up a carrot to the "pretty pony," who happened to be me.

Grandma laughed and called her long dead brother, Al, to come and see the pretty piebald pony standing on the porch in search of carrots or some grain. She told Al, "I call my pony 'Tsa-ni' for a friend I used to know," and beckoned to me softly, "Tsa-niiiii..."

I said, "It's Laurel, Grandma, not a pony," and she chortled skeptically as if I were a foolish child.

She lay down on her bed, which was right beside the window, and talked until she drifted off to sleep. "Did Dad and I ever tell you about John? He was just the best friend the either of us ever had." Her face was softly lit by the corner streetlight, peaceful looking now, at rest. "His Indian name was Tsa-ni."

Tsa-ni. John. It had been so many years since I had thought of John and the cemetery. For just a moment I slipped back in time to see my grandpa smiling at a younger, plumper Grandma at John's grave. I got caught up in memories of the way life used to be when we three were together. A shiver ran along my spine as those memories led to others. My knees were shaking as I went down Grandma's steps and headed home. An odd sensation overcame me, a sense of revelation or perhaps hope.

I only lived a couple blocks away from Grandma, and hurried home to finish the half-started poem while my feelings were still strong. It seems strange in looking back that my sadness over losing Grandma could begin a healing in me. I didn't want to lose my grandma, not at any age. It seemed wrong that experiencing first hand my Grandma's failing mind and body should benefit me. Somehow, in knowing about the voices Grandma heard and the visions she saw, my life began to get on track again.

Voices

Fearsome energy reserves—
a vast creative force—
were centered at the heart of her
until there came a hole inside her
large enough to drive a truck through.
What made that hole,
no one will ever know,
especially her.
First went the heart and soul of her,
and then the once quick mind
began to slowly drift to some elusive
God-forsaken limbo of defeat
repleat with dark hallucinations
of her past and present life.
She couldn't find her way back,
had to learn to live there amidst voices,
shadows, sad imaginings,
and memories that represent
a twisted version of the truth.
What vicious demon of disease,
what harsh genetic or familial tendency
has forced her to that place
where she sees horses, long dead brothers,
and hears voices from a now forgotten past?

This poem, also, went into my favorite Bible with the one I wrote for Mom. The words were forgotten as soon as I put them to paper. I didn't reread it or notice the terminology I'd used, didn't realize that it could have been me I wrote about. I fell into exhaustion on the bed beside my husband and through what remained of night I dreamed of Grandpa.

Grandpa giving me a mock "Dutch-rub," atop my head. Grandpa laughing and smiling that big warm smile of his. Grandpa lounging happily in some sunny place alive with waving grasses, talking with another man whose burnished face was glowing with a joyful smile. The man with Grandpa looked familiar, like I ought to know him.

That night I slept the sweetest sleep I'd had in years.

Part Two

Intaglios

Somewhere, etched beneath the surface
unseen, encased in tender flesh,
a silent history of life conceals itself
from prying eyes.
And hidden deep inside my mind
exists a cavern full of memories
quite carefully excised and isolated
from the rest—disguised,
diluted by deliberate denial.
I am the craftsman of these hieroglyphics.
Only I can translate what they mean.
Intaglios of my own inspired creation—
carvings, sweet incisions, gentle gashes—
were created over time in guise of self protection
that I never really needed.
Intaglios lie in hiding,
bas relief and throbbing out my story
once the acid of my tears has washed them clean.
I wonder which of these I'll be—
frigid marble, crystal, living flesh, or glass—
and what will be the secret message of intaglios
when the story ends?
God is the only one who knows.

Chapter Six

Herb and Esther

1989 was not a banner year by any stretch of the imagination, but some good did come of it. That year I started thinking and reasoning again, began the seeking phase of my dilemma, and finally stopped wallowing in self-pity. I started looking back over my life, and vowed because of that retrospective not to waste the time I had left with Grandma as I had with Mom and Grandpa. If I seem to dwell on this period of time more than others, it's because my grandma's final months of life were especially enlightening to me. In watching her die and listening as she relived her life, I somehow evolved beyond my self-inflicted misery.

The timeline of events was rather frightening in review, but I forced myself to contemplate what could be remembered of it. My slow withdrawal from reality had begun in 1980.

That final visit with Grandma and Grandpa to put flowers on John's grave had been in 1981. Grandpa died in 1982 and Mom in 1984. And I had reached 1989 with Grandma in the nursing home and me still dragging on not showing much improvement over nine years' time.

It was a humbling thing to realize that, even in her demented state, Grandma was a stronger, more courageous soul than I had been, those past nine years.

She loved to share her memories, the joys and sorrows she

had known in over ninety years of living, so I listened and attempted to remember everything she said. Although Grandma's mind was wandering, stuck in some other place and time, her stories were remarkable. Her voice had become weak and tremulous, no longer resonant and confident the way it had been once. She actively hallucinated, but oh what wondrous tales she told as her mind wandered! I sat beside her bed and clutched a bony twisted hand, pretending to be anyone or anything she thought I was at any given time.

Sometimes I was her brother Al, sometimes a piebald pony standing by the "fence," as she called her bedrail. At other times I would be Grandpa giving her a kiss upon the cheek or forehead. She would turn her face up to me so tenderly, as if to reach a tall man for a kiss, and smile like she was twenty and in love again. My lips would softly brush her wrinkled cheek or forehead and she'd laugh a little laugh and say, "Oh Herb." My mind's eye can still recall that laugh and see the sweet flirtatious smile that crossed her face. My lips still feel that dry crinkly skin beneath them whenever I think about her, and I treasure that remembrance.

Grandma talked about the early times of knowing Herb as if I had been a part of it. Her mind would wander to her father's farm in Iowa where first she spotted Herb. She wanted to be pretty for him, wanted to wear makeup, but her father wouldn't allow it, not for the likes of Herb who was a farm hand out of Kansas. Grandma sneaked and rubbed a little rouge on her cheeks and lips anyway, thinking it made her look older than her sixteen years.

Herb seemed quite a dashing figure to her, six years older and almost rakish when he got dressed up to go to town. It shocked her almost breathless when he dubbed the dress up hat he wore his "go to hell hat." He'd cock it sassily down over one eye and grin that big wide grin of his while piling in the wagon and heading off to town. What a romantic figure he must have been in those days, strong from lifting bales and other heavy farm work, taller head and shoulders than her short and stocky brothers.

Grandma painted clear and colorful word pictures of Grandpa and those early times they shared while they were courting, as she called it.

Her dementia made the stories Grandma told me seem more charming, somehow, as I struggled to record them. My mind was still muddled in 1989. I couldn't remember details very well, so I wrote things down on bits and scraps of paper, then put them in my Bible for safe keeping. Poems or random bits of prose often came to me after visiting Grandma at the nursing home. Most days I couldn't wait til reaching home to write them down and would scribble them on paper in the car.

One evening, Grandma told what she called the "apple" story for the hundredth time. The apple story hadn't meant much to me in the past, or else I had forgotten it entirely.

This night, she made a circle with her fingers to describe the apple. Her face was creased so sweetly with a joyous smile as Grandma told the story of her wedding apple. She told of Herb and their elopement, their wedding trip to Kansas on the train, and of the present purchased proudly by her new husband. She described the passenger car they rode in so clearly that I could feel the swaying movement of it and hear the clacking sound made by the train wheels.

She detailed their sharing of the wedding apple so distinctly that I could smell its fragrance and taste its juicy sweetness. Her eyes lit up with such delight that it was clear she thought the wedding apple was a precious and romantic gift beyond compare. I can still see her face and hear her trembling voice each time I think of it. That Grandma could recall her joy with such clarity, even in the throes of her dementia, was an odd comfort to me in 1989.

The apple story always began with the early days of their courtship, and from there would progress to their elopement and the apple. In the telling of her story, Grandma always called my grandpa "Herb." Initially, he enthralled her with his eyes of clearest blue that twinkled merrily each time he laughed or got the better of her with his gentle mischief. Grandma was smitten with him and everybody knew it, especially Herb, who had set out to win her with a vengeance.

Herb had come to Iowa from Kansas late in August with the harvest crew, not realizing that a whole new way of life would open to him. Grandma laughed each time she told it, how she flirted, how she set her cap for Herb and got him just the way she planned it out in secret. She loved to tell how openly she defied her father; who forbid her having anything to do with Herb and his "Kansas ways." I can only imagine what effect she must have had on Grandpa back then, with her short stature and tiny waist, casting saucy glances his way at every turn.

He worked hard, this strong and tall man, with a purpose.

At first Herb didn't think he had a snowball's chance in summer of marrying a rich man's daughter. He doubted if transporting her away from one life to another back to Kansas as his bride was possible. He didn't have to labor very hard to win her as it turned out. He had Grandma's full cooperation!

One sunny day he grinned at Esther's brothers and said they might as well accept it, he was marrying their baby sister. And that was that.

At this point in Grandma's story she would tell of their elopement, how Herb took her on the train from Iowa to Kansas and bought her one huge apple, sweet and red, for them to share as they began their life together. To them that apple was a symbol and the sweet accentuation of their vows. Gnarled fingers formed the largest circle in the air each time she told the apple story, and her eyes would sparkle with the knowledge that their lives together had lasted seven decades and beyond.

That story and the other reminiscences my grandma shared sparked the beginning of renewal in me. Renewed belief in the power of love, renewed hope for my future, and the first stirrings of spiritual rebirth began that final time she told the apple story. I wept to think of the day their shining eyes first met and of the way she cried and whispered "Herb" the day his clouded eyes were dimmed and closed in death. I cried and blew my runny nose and kept on listening.

Their love and long relationship was far from idyllic. Grandma would have been the first to say so. Their self-described financial status in those early years was one step above dirt poor. They struggled every way a couple can back in the days when almost everyone was poor. They worked in exchange for a roof over their heads, worked from sun up to sun down for fifty cents to buy some flour and sugar or a bit of coffee for their breakfast. And when their babies came along they both worked harder. Huge plots of vegetables were grown, tended, and canned over open fires in brutal Kansas heat to lay in food for winter. All this was in addition to their other daily labors, which began at daylight and ended when they both fell into bed exhausted.

It wasn't always easy, not romantic, but they didn't care.

They loved each other for the long haul the way a married couple ought to. Every bit and piece of Grandma's rambling stories punctuated that belief. She was old, but hadn't always been, and could still remember what it was like to be in love.

Grandma looked at me and laughed one day, not long before she died, and said, "You know, I can't believe it when I realize how old I am. In my heart and mind I still feel eighteen." She was in an awful state of neglect by then.

Her knees were stiff and swollen from inactivity despite the exercises done several times a day. The hair she'd always kept so "cute and curly" as she called it was unkempt and thinning, and no amount of combing could correct it.

Her duster was quite dirty because she wouldn't let anyone change it or give her a decent bath. She was in a state of nearly terminal starvation because she was too paranoid to eat or drink. Nearly everything was poisoned to her way of thinking. The doctor said she could be force fed in the hospital or rehydrated with intravenous fluids, but her heart was giving out and all her bodily functions were failing. She was 91, so the decision was made by her family to let her pass on naturally, without heroic interventions.

I went home crying every night to see her in such a condition. Grandma had always told me we were "pals." She'd always whispered it as if we had a juicy secret no one else could share. I didn't weep and rage at God the way I had in other years, with other losses. I simply cried in secret and in silence at the loss of someone so dear to me. I'd never been able to cry easily or freely, but I remembered Grandma saying tears are how God cleans out our eyes and soothes our heartaches. So I cried.

Her memories of Grandpa and their life together triggered recollections of my own. Grandpa was the one who patiently and calmly taught me how to drive on ice and snow. He taught me how to drive a stick shift good as any man could, and beamed his pride with each improvement. It was Grandpa who taught me mini lessons when I went out into the world and started working. Grandpa drove me back and forth to school and work and each trip was a lesson in the making.

I didn't appreciate his lessons as much as I should have in those days. "Be nice to people." he would say while nodding sagely. "No matter what they do to you, be nice." Or, "Don't pay any mind to what people say about you or the way you look. There's nothing wrong with how you look. Just do your best." Or, "Don't start drinkin', Honey, like your dad does. Enough hearts have been broken over things like that." Grandpa filled two jobs with all us kids, but more so with me since I was oldest. He was Grandpa, first and foremost, but he also became father when he had to. I didn't value his kind heart and simple logic like I should have while I had him in my life. That's why I had to think about him and the many ways he influenced me while waiting for the ending of my Grandma's life.

That same day she talked of feeling eighteen, Grandma clutched my hand as if it was a life raft. She didn't know who I was for sure, but something in me must have looked familiar. She didn't talk much that day. Once she croaked, "I didn't used to be this old and useless."

Another time she smiled and said, "I used to make such lovely doughnuts. I specialized in doughnuts." While drifting in and out of sleep she rambled incoherently about John and graves, and finally said one word, "Herb."

It was clear from how she looked and sounded that Grandma wouldn't be with me for much longer. It didn't take much medical training to know that she was dying.

I looked at this fine woman in her dying state, then went straight home to write the words I thought she might have written if she were able. The next morning before heading off to work, I taped a shortened version of her story to the door of Grandma's room.

The poem represented more than ninety years of a life that had been fully and richly lived, complete with all the joys and sorrows humans know. Grandma's life, like everyone's, had been made up of little things that somehow came together as a whole. I don't know if anyone read it, but I felt a little better thinking someone might have.

My Name is Esther Clara

Esther–age 91

Once I was young, sturdy and strong,
dreaming of a life to call my own.
I helped my mother on the farm—
a clean and lovely farm in Iowa.
We baked and cleaned and washed
and fed the men. Our work was hard.
Mom liked pretty plants and flowers,
embroidered linens, keeping house,
and so do I. At least I did when I was able.
One year a tall young man from Kansas
came to work the farms around in harvest.
He was so strong, with such a sense of humor,
and to my way of thinking he was just the kind of man I wanted
for a husband and the father of my children.
Oh yes, I got in trouble with my father

for flirting with that Kansas boy,
who wasn't even Lutheran, not rich,
without one hope of ever being landed gentry.
I didn't care. Herb married me
and took me back to Kansas on a train.
I wish you could have seen me then,
so plump and smart and capable,
independent with a mind of my own.
Looking at me now you wouldn't think that would you?
Looking at me now you'd never guess that I was married,
raised a family, ran my household with an iron hand,
cooked and cleaned with proud abandon,
baked bread and specialized in making doughnuts,
loved my children, and later on
a couple generations more of my descendants.
That life was not so long ago.
The years flew by so fast I scarcely noticed,
and somewhere deep inside my mind I still remember.
One day you're young and strong, the next you're old.
Remember that—you whose legs still carry you
from place to place, whose eyes and ears still see and hear,
whose minds are clear, who think your lives have just begun.
It really wasn't all that long ago.

Grandma died not long after that in the fall of 1989. Like I said earlier, it was not a banner year by any stretch of the imagination. I had reached a strange sense of peace about her dying, and felt a tiny spark of joy inside, almost. She went to rest next to my grandpa, close to Mother. I told myself that somewhere in the heavens, maybe Grandma was happy again.

Herb and Esther

I hadn't reached the stage of thinking that the circle of their lives had been completed in a happy place, but I was close to that and getting closer.

Chapter Seven

Mea Culpa

I had a co-worker once who muttered "mea culpa" repeatedly throughout her work shift. That used to seem strange, and even amusing to me, until the need arose to struggle with some "mea culpa" issues of my own.

Recurring thoughts of suicide or sudden death haunted me as I began a fearsome period of self-examination. Memories were all I had left of Grandma, Grandpa, and Mom, but with the time preceding Grandma's passing, all desire to practice the occult had ended.

My favorite Bible stayed on the shelf unread, its pages crammed with poems and scraps of paper full of scribbled memories and thoughts. I faced each day one moment at a time and searched for answers that were slow in coming. I was slowly healing but not healed, not whole despite my searching. Here is what I learned from another year of contemplation.

My troubled times had been preceded by a period where I stopped focusing on the positive and beautiful and began to dwell on the negative. As a result, my brain somehow imploded with the stress of living in a world I saw as being full of injustices and pain. Too many young people died untapped while cruel despots thrived. Too many good women like my mother struggled to survive while others I considered less deserving prospered. I blamed it all on God when that world took what gifts I had to offer and did not provide the expected returns on my investments.

To blame God is a common trait in humans, I think, but we put different labels on it. We don't call it "blaming." We call it burnout, road rage, going ballistic, losing it, but it all boils down to the fact that we stop believing in and relying on God to help us through. At least, that's what I did.

In my case, I held on far beyond my limits til the day my brain decided to shut down a bit. Since I no longer set parameters my mind could live with, it ended the battle quite decisively without my conscious input. Everyone was shocked when that happened, especially me. I had always seen myself as strong, invincible, and capable of winning every fight. I was foolish to ignore all the warning signs my mind and body tried to give me over time. I was mistaken to damper down my spiritual beliefs and focus all my rage on God. I raged until my whole life crumbled like a wad of paper someone threw into the trash. It was hard accepting that I had been the sole architect of my misfortune.

During the time when I was lost, it felt like all the pathways in my brain were unconnected, misfiring. I searched for simple logic and emotions, explanations that would help me find my way, but they were gone or hiding in the underbrush that was my mind. I was dead to all emotion, dry inside. Of everyone who hated how I was in those days, I hated it the most because it wasn't me. The real me was athletic, sweet of nature, not unkind. The real me loved her family and friends, adored her husband, saw all nature as a blessing. If only I had cried, "God help me!" before I threw it all away and had to struggle back alone.

I must confess to thinking that dementia had set in early in life. My reasoning for thinking that was because, during those dark years, the world and many people in it seemed mysterious and frightening. I'd been a nurse for twenty years or more, but suddenly the smell of blood and the sight of bleeding people left me dazed and sickened. Traumatic injuries and medical emergencies became horrifying paralyzing situations that I could no longer manage capably.

I no longer had the confidence, ability, or skill to face my daily life as a nurse or a woman whole and strong.

I did still love my husband, family and friends, but that love hid and had to be forced out into daylight. I did grieve and cry, but not with tears that anyone could see.

Finally, in striving to overcome my failings, I drained myself of every ounce of strength.

No one had to point these revelations out to me. I learned them all the hard way by battling my way through them on my own. I waged war on weakness and defeat but stubbornly held on to sadness, and to disappointment in the God of my younger years. That God no longer seemed real to me. It is a testament to His faithfulness, not mine, that I began to understand the true cause of my troubles.

Chapter Eight

Ancestry and Friends

I never gave a lot of thought to my ancestry before 1990.

Oh, I knew my grandma and grandpa were of German descent and remembered hearing that my dad's side of the family was Scot-Irish, English, and Cherokee. None of that seemed important to me. Ancestry and genetic tendencies were non-essential information to my way of thinking. It was only after I had reached the "seeking" phase that family history became important.

The only way I knew to begin the healing process was to dredge up what old memories I could and then examine them for clues to what had made me the person I once was. Before my family and friends could understand my time of trouble, I had to figure out the scope of what I'd lost. I began with the earliest times I could remember, recalling people, places, and situations that had impressed me as a youngster.

Collecting those lost bits and pieces of memories, looking back, turned out to be a wonderful journey.

I remembered living in a tiny house that Mom shared with her sister, Maxine, while both their husbands were at war in far off places. They kept a flock of chickens in their fenced back yard and every chicken had a name. They used to cry each time they had to kill and eat one of their chickens. Grandpa was too soft-hearted to "do the deed" as Mom called it, so Grandma always had to kill the chickens for them.

Our tiny house was crowded with the three of us, and two white dogs by name of Daisy June, and Mitzi. Daisy June was fatter, Mitzi smarter, and both were pets that I considered mine, along with chickens whose names I have forgotten.

I had two responsibilities in those days. One was sitting still while Mother rolled my hair in ringlets that she thought made me look just like Shirley Temple. My other job was to squeeze and bust the little ball of orange dye that stained the awful stuff they called margarine in those days. Those were the WAR years, the BIG war as Mother called it, so we couldn't have real butter. Sugar and coffee were limited, and gas was rationed too. It was in that initial three years of my life that I learned the lessons of compassion, loving people and animals, sharing and sacrifice to further common good.

When the war had ended, after Dad and Uncle Kenny returned home safely, I remember spending a lot of time with Aunt Maxine and Uncle Kenny. Aunt Maxine was a Registered Nurse who remained a friend and comforting presence throughout my life. Uncle Kenny was a red-headed Irishman with a blustering temper and a big loving heart. Those years right after World War Two remain mostly blank to this day, except for random happy moments. Remembering, it seemed like yesterday that we were riding down to Kansas City late at night to see Uncle Kenny's mother. I was standing on the seat between them because my knees were scuffed and sore from falling and it hurt to bend them. The murmur of their voices talking to each other is still clear to me these many decades later, and a comfort when I stopped to think about it. I was everybody's baby in those days, blessed, protected and loved. What a pity I'd forgotten for a time being loved in such abundance by so many different people!

And I remembered going to the river on a picnic with my Uncle Don, Aunt Carol, and their lifelong friends, Earl and Ginny Elliott. The air was warm and hazy like most summer days are in Kansas. They were young married couples back then, so much in love, but still willing to include me in their day. By that time I'd been transformed from what had once been petite and pretty to what I call my fat and clumsy stage of life. I tried so hard to be ladylike, but ended up falling or somehow scattering sand all over the picnic lunch or blanket that entire day. It mortified me to be so clumsy, even at that young age, because Don and Carol were my heroes and I had a childhood crush on Earl.

Despite my klutzy contributions to their day, they all forgave my clumsiness for fear of wounding me. That summer afternoon with them taught me something important. If you love someone, you will overlook and forgive their foibles and shortcomings, like they did mine.

Right about that same age my mother looked at me one day as if she were quite puzzled, and finally said I was just like my Cherokee great grandmother, "old" when I was born. Why this particular memory surfaced when I can't remember other things is anybody's guess. It was strange for her to say that, because to my knowledge no one in my mother's generation had ever met my dad's Native grandmother.

I can't offer any clearer explanation of that statement.

Mom was right, I suppose, as only mothers can be when they try to figure out what makes their children tick. I was often quiet, stoic, lost in thought, and seldom showed my feelings even as a child. Perhaps I WAS old when I was born. I hope to ask her what she meant by that some day when we meet face to face again.

I remained the only niece and grandchild for several years before my siblings and our cousins came along. We older kids grew up together, with me the oldest, and shared a mostly happy childhood. Frequently, those carefree times were spent on Uncle Jerome's farm. He had married Mom's younger sister, Aunt Lois, and their farm was just a few miles west and north of the town where I grew up. We kids got into all kinds of trouble, terrorized the cattle and the poor old gelding horse named Midnight. Uncle Jerome would just whistle and go on about his business, but Aunt Lois would crack down on our shenanigans if she caught us. She worried, of course, that one of us would get hurt or worse.

One day those fears of hers became reality when my sister Jeanne fell into their septic tank, which was an open pit in those days. I can still see Aunt Lois clearly, apron flying up around her head, as she jumped feet first into the septic tank. She didn't hesitate one second, merely plunged into that putrid water, while everybody else amongst us, including the adults, stood screaming helplessly. We all expected death to come to Jeanne at any moment, but Aunt Lois thrashed about in that foul water til she managed to retrieve her. The bravery and selflessness of that act became another lesson to me as I thought back on it. No one ever thanked her for it quite enough, I fear.

By my early childhood we had become a large extended family that celebrated all the different ways families do. I have struggled to remember, vaguely, Christmas dinners, Sunday dinners, Easter baskets, Easter outfits, and going off to church on Sunday mornings dressed as fancily as Mother could afford. One thing I clearly could recall was that every family dinner was begun with “The Lord’s Prayer” and sung as only Uncle Jerome could sing it. No other voice conveyed the spirit and emotion he derived from singing, and so when he passed on it didn’t seem so strange at all to hear him sing at his own funeral. Aunt Lois played a tape of his angelic voice to send him off to glory on the day that he was buried.

I could not remember much about my Dad’s side of the family no matter how hard I tried. Grandma Smith had dark snapping eyes and strong cheekbones, like her mother, and was a blunt no-nonsense woman. Grandpa Smith was English, short of stature, balding and mild-mannered. They lived a simple frugal life and died when I was young. We had a full complement of relatives from both sides of their family, but my memories of them are fragmented at best. My dad took after his mother’s side of the family with native coloring predominant. His hair was black as raven’s wings and he looked bronze in every season. He was a striking, handsome man, given to frightening drunken rages. Dad left my life when I was nine and Mom divorced him.

In looking back, I realized how great a part my relatives had played in my upbringing as a child. It was as if each one of them contributed a small part to my thinking, my beliefs. I learned lessons from them all, beginning in my infancy, progressing through my youth and well into adulthood. My ancestry had made me what I was, with all my weak and strong points. I was the product of many generations that had lived and loved before me.

I could see it clearly while sorting through the family pictures that went back as far as antique tintypes and stark old photographs in black and white. The faces in those pictures reflected dour practicality, quick wit, and eyes alight with humor. Relatives I'd known or heard about were said to have a bookish bent, or to be compulsive, driven to achieving what they hoped to gain from life. That was but one part of my familial tendencies. Pictured also were spirits dark with hints of bygone clans and tribes.

Dark flashing eyes, ripe with dreaming and hoping, revealed their secrets to the camera. In me, the traces of their legacy lived on. Quick minds and unsung heroes wedded Celts who practiced witchcraft and believed in ancient magic dark and fearsome. Simple farmers and devoted Christians fell in love with native women of the plains.

In ages past my people danced to Celtic rhythms or they donned the eagle feather and the paint of battle as they struggled to survive. I was the progeny of many generations.

Ancient bloods had mixed within my ancestors and relatives to make us what we had become as people. We were made up of true geniuses and poets, sad dreamers, warriors and Christians, all molded and connected by the imprints that lived on inside our minds. A little part of them still lived in me. Just realizing that taught me a lot about myself.

The friends who stayed beside me through all my years of madness were and are the truest sort of people, the kind we all should cherish and give thanks for. Every one of them had trials of their own to contend with, jobs and families, financial worries, struggles, but they all stayed loyal to me. They supported me with love and understanding. They forgave my foolish whims and fractured thoughts. They all loved me, even when their patience was stretched thin, and when I hurt them with my cold and distant behavior.

I learned in seeking answers and in looking back that the beautiful thing about friendship is that it didn't fail when I went wrong.

My friends were like my husband, like my family. They loved me even when I didn't seem to love them back. They loved me in the bad times when I didn't know their names or recognize their faces. They loved me twenty or thirty years ago and love me now with constancy.

My friends have always been the best of everything a friend could ever be. In dreams and while awake, they're with me as a constant reassurance. They've always been there to share whatever energy they have to help me realize my hopes and dreams. Each one of them has taught me different lessons.

Friends helped me to learn courage in the face of sorrow, helped me bear my sadness for awhile until I became strong enough to make my way again. They helped convince me I was worthy of respect and love by letting that light shine within their eyes until I could believe what they were saying. Friends taught me how to laugh again when I believed such laughter was impossible for me.

Friends helped me to become a stronger, less despairing person who could face the world again. They helped me grow. And through it all they asked me nothing of myself except to love them and accept them as my friends.

I retraced these fragments of my life reluctantly at first. Regaining lost ground is not always easy. But when this exercise was finished, I knew for certain that I had been richly blessed.

Loving relatives had nurtured me since birth. They taught me compassion and forgiveness, taught me how to love without strings or chains, instilled in me the values that should have lasted me a lifetime. My friends had carried on in that tradition by demonstrating loyalty and love, regardless of whether I deserved that generosity.

In short, they were all a godsend to me. How could I have lost perspective on that, even for a moment?

Chapter Nine

Places

I had always loved nature and the outdoor world. In those grand athletic days before I lost my mind, I walked two miles a day come rain or shine or blowing snow. I loved the woods along the river by the town where I grew up and the wild creatures living in that shelter belt of trees.

I loved the crisp fresh scent of winter air and the way hot winds would blow across the prairies where I lived. I loved my home town and everything about it, from the brick streets to the way it lay spread out along the river. Even those joys left me in the trying times while I was lost.

Before that awful time, I always found some beauty everywhere I went. Every state and town seemed blessed with different attributes I could enjoy. For the sake of simplicity, I began my backward exploration with the town where I grew up. It was an old railroad town in northern Kansas, called Marysville, but in my mind I always thought of it by its original name of Palmetto.

The Blue River curves gently through the valley there, and in the green breast of her bottomlands lie the roots of my youth. There, the scent of prairie grass and sweet clover on the wind came to me as a sudden gift on summer days. There, the bright blue sky is met with greenish hue of trees and corn, or browns of rich earth and fertile valley lighted by the summer sun. I used to stand transfixed and breathe it in, absorb the sight of it while thinking how it must have looked when only native tribes enjoyed such bounty. But that simple native life was many moons ago, long before there was a town called first Palmetto, later Marysville.

Long dead founding fathers in their day chose to name the town Palmetto for the native grasses growing there, green and chest high on a tallish man. Palmetto sounded so exotic to them, so important somehow, as a symbol of American resilience and strength.

Palmetto. It was to be a portal to the very kind of life that every man hoped for, a site of great importance. Only goodness, purity, and virtue would reside there, they were certain of it. Only the honorable and reputable would survive there in such a clean and blessed place. Surely no manner of evil or corruption could reach them or abide there. No dregs of their society could ever make a way there to desecrate the prairie bastion that Palmetto would become.

Life was good there in Palmetto. Eventually, the native tribes were forced to scatter on the four winds in desperation as more travelers from Europe and the east sought and found Palmetto. Decades passed, and then a century and more. All the while some good did grow there as the founding fathers planned it, along with evil and corruption thriving quietly within it as it does in every city, every town.

I was horrified to reach my middle years and see beyond the picture perfect town I once had glorified in thought and verse. How very immature of me to think that any place could be that perfect! That childish disappointment in a place and people helped contribute to my madness for awhile. These days, however, I can look back with clearer vision and separate the good things from the bad.

I still love Palmetto, even though I've chosen not to live there anymore. I've learned to love my memories of it, like the way it hugs the river with blue cobalt sky above it and the prairie land around it rich with life. I love the ancestors it gave me, for their dreams live on inside me as I catch the scent of prairie grass, sweet clover, and an ancient past inhabiting the winds that blow across Palmetto.

How can one who knew such beauty in the places she had been believe that God is dead or non-existent? I had reached the point where I could at least ask myself that question without fearing what God's answer might be. With that thought in mind, I proceeded through a mental list of places I had visited or lived. I've never had the opportunity to travel much and don't remember many of the places I have been.

The Kansas and Nebraska prairies have been clearly fixed in my mind because I spent most of my life there. The Mississippi River valley is an awesome sight when viewed from rocky overlooks near where my sister used to live in Hannibal, Missouri. Centre County, Pennsylvania enthralled me with its early American history and lush forested mountains. But mostly I remember Kerby Knob, Kentucky. It's as different from my prairie home as any place could possibly be. I was blessed to live on Kerby Knob twice in my lifetime and to visit there many times.

It's located in Jackson County where my husband was born and raised. Every time on Kerby Knob, for me, was like experiencing a rare treasure.

A winding road that passes through "the Knob," as locals

call it, has an overhang of hardwood trees that provide deep shade in summer. Driving through the Knob for the first time, and every time thereafter, my breath was taken by the heavy pungent odor of moist earth. Such earth can only be transformed from leaves that fell throughout millennia past.

A sense of ancientness pervaded every moment that I lived on Kerby Knob. With every rising of the milkish fog at morning, I could feel my spirits soaring to embrace the day at hand. And by evening we would sit on our front porch to watch the ghostly settling of fog around us. It progressed like spirit fingers, grasping at the hollers just at dusk. Any descriptive term I try to use is inadequate.

You have to see it for yourself to understand the power wielded by that Appalachian fog. To stand outside in it at night while opaque moisture swirls around your face is magical!

Rock-bottomed creeks run clear and cold there, flanked by rugged cliffs and forests. Such water comes from deep down in the mountains where no man has seen its source since time began. Wild mountain laurel and hibiscus grow in such profusion that the human mind can scarce absorb the sight.

I always called those mountains "God's Creation" because His hand was so in evidence around me there, regardless of the season.

A different kind of nature song was sung there than the music of my native plains, but no less sweet—a song of Kerby Knob and Red Lick, Sand Gap, Big Hill Mountain. All of these were so far distant from the Sand Hills, Flint Hills, and the broad flat river valleys of my familiar prairie home. A part of me will always be there, spirits rising with the morning fog. It sounds trite for me to say this, but my heart has been forever captured by those ancient tree topped mountains. I will always love my Appalachian home on Kerby Knob.

Chapter Ten

Grass Dance

By the mid-1990s I had been evading God's presence for fifteen years or more. Almost ten of those years had been wasted exploring occult means of treating madness and despair. Those wasted years resulted in bitterness and cynicism. Another half a decade had been spent in seeking some other solution to that madness. Finally, I could feel my life was taking on a new direction, clearer focus. It was sheer stupidity of me to waste so many years before facing the truth.

The catalyst that brought about my sudden turning back to God was quite unexpected. I have never spoken of this happening because just about everyone I know would have thought me certifiably crazy if I had. Who could blame them if they thought I'd lost my grip again? They had survived my actively hallucinating for years. They had sighed and carried on when I drove halfway cross the country in a less-than-lucid state. Who amongst them wouldn't chalk up this experience to my imagination or hallucination? I had spent so many years not knowing the real from the imaginary, living in a shadow world that no one else could see. I cannot blame my friends and family if they should doubt that my miracle is real.

My miracle went exactly as I write it now. Not sort of like it or a little bit like it, but exactly as it is recorded.

Thinking of that day still gives me goose bumps because the wonder of it, even now, amazes me.

That afternoon I'd laid curled up on the bed staring out my bedroom window, watching tree limbs as they stirred in the breeze. Their gentle movement and the soft sound of rustling leaves lulled me off to sleep. Sometime later I began to dream that the phone was ringing. In my dream, I was so drowsy, so at peace, that I didn't want to disturb my slumber to answer the call. While still in a dreaming state, I reluctantly crawled out of bed and reached for the phone. I could hear pleasant, peaceful sounding music in the background as I said, "Hello."

It was the so-familiar rumble of my grandpa's voice on the line, all choked up with emotion like it used to get when he was sad or happy. His voice was trembling with elation when he said my name, as if he had some wonderful news to share with me.

"Laurel! John's right here beside me and he said to tell you... GRASS DANCE!"

I answered him sleepily, and felt no surprise at all to be getting a phone call from my dead grandpa. "Grandpa, is that really YOU?"

I could hear soft murmuring voices in the background along with that happy sounding music of no particular genre. The closest I can come to a description of the music is that it sounded like a thousand gently tinkling wind chimes of varying sizes and tones. The sound of it tickled pleasantly at my ear, traveled to my brain and down my spine. It was as if a softly warming electrical current crackled gently through me for a moment as I waited for Grandpa's reply.

His answer was to say again, a little more insistently this time. "John...says...tell...you...grass..." then, "Oh..."

I could hear his frustration, and strained to glean some meaning from the cryptic message Grandpa was laboring to communicate. The sound was fading slowly from his voice and from the background music. I was almost frantic by then, thinking Grandpa would call me from beyond the grave and talk about something as unimportant as grass.

"GRASS DANCE." Grandpa raised his voice a notch with those two words.

"And one more thing Sorrel Top, John said to tell you that a man's days are like the grass..." (Sorrel Top! Grandpa was the only one who ever called me that! How many years had passed since he had called me Sorrel Top?)

That was it. No goodbyes or I love you's could be spoken.

The connection ended suddenly, and just as abruptly, I woke up. A big smile was spreading on my face from ear to ear and I felt warm inside and out, like I was floating in a thick, tepid liquid. The joy I felt was nearly suffocating for a moment.

There are people who will tell me this experience was nothing more than dreaming. Others are bound to be convinced that it was a hallucination or simply wishful thinking. People who have known me since childhood will tell me that I missed my Grandpa and subconsciously imagined his voice. I know better. That phone call in my dream was God reaching out to one of His fallen, obstinate children.

God reached out for my attention in a way He knew would surely work, by using Grandpa and a subject that was certain to intrigue me. God used Grandpa and his old friend John to bring me back where I belonged.

I've given considerable thought to this dream. It would not have had the same effect if it had been anyone but Grandpa on the phone. His voice and the emotions, so apparent when he spoke, were a familiar memory, a part of me. His relationship with John was deep and lasting in life. It seemed logical to me that it would be the same in death.

Only Grandpa, Grandpa's voice, with John at his side, would have made that dream believable to me.

Dreams and visions sent from God need no interpretation. I didn't need to call a pastor or seek counseling to understand the message. All the clues I needed would be found within the Bible, and in knowing what John meant when he said "grass dance."

God doesn't give up on us either. When He sets a thing in motion, it continues with momentum. I didn't have to leave the house or leaf through an encyclopedia to learn about the grass dance. While the dream was still fresh in my mind, a program came on one of the educational channels that told me everything I needed to know. One day I simply turned on the TV and there it was.

The full meaning of the grass dance and its true origination, have been lost in time, the narrator intoned, but historians believe it to be quite ancient. Legend has it that the native Omaha people were the first to practice grass dancing, and over time its use spread southward to the other plains tribes.

The purpose of grass dancing was a simple one. The plains were rich with waving grasses far as the eye could see in those days. Grasses waved in the direction of the wind; they bent but were unbroken by winds that blew across the prairies.

The movement was fluid, bendable, and grass appeared to dance when viewed with eyes attuned to what the earth was saying. That dancing prairie grass spoke of strength and grace, of spirit gone unbent before strong wind and all the forces wind could muster.

Several strands of braided grass hung almost to the dancers' knees and every movement caused a gentle swaying of each braid to and fro. First the ancients danced before the buffalo preparing for a hunt, for what purpose no one can be certain. And later, dancers circled, bent, and swayed in sinuous rhythm as they trampled down the prairie grass in preparation for a tribal gathering or pow wow.

There was a purpose to their dancing, one that helped them make sense out of lives that often could be unpredictable and harsh.

I liked the sound and thought of it. "Spirit gone unbent before strong wind and all the forces wind could muster."

Perhaps that was the message John had sent me from beyond the grave with God's and Grandpa's help. I had been badly bent but was not broken? I was stronger than I seemed to be? Stronger than I thought I was?

The Bible speaks of grass in several places. The allusion is that grass represents life's fleeting nature and man's vulnerability to forces beyond his control. John quoted from the Psalms and the prophet Isaiah when he said, "A man's days are like the grass..." Yes, I did remember that John had never learned to read during his life on earth, so he had to quote the Bible from another source.

I believe John heard that quote from the same source the unschooled psalmist and prophet Isaiah heard it. I believed it then, and continue to believe it now, that those words came directly from God's mouth to John. John heard those words from his Creator and passed them on to me.

I was certain that God had reached out to me through Grandpa and his good friend John in a dream. That dream did not fade with waking like so many dreams do. I was re-energized, reborn, rejuvenated and repentant seconds after waking from the dream. I refocused on the good and set about immediately to rid myself of all the evil trappings I'd allowed to taint my life.

It's hard telling what the neighbors thought if they were watching what I did in my back yard that day. I dug the deepest hole I could manage with a spading fork, which was all I had to dig with. The hole was four feet wide and nearly three feet deep. Armload after armload of occult paraphernalia and the raging thoughts I'd put to paper were carried to that hole and dumped there. All was thoroughly doused with charcoal starter. Before putting a match to it, I looked towards the heavens and said a tearful prayer out loud. I didn't care if the neighbors heard me because my prayer needed saying.

"Dear Lord, forgive my foolishness and blasphemy. In Jesus' name I pray for your forgiveness. Please reclaim me as your child and redirect my life to some worthy purpose."

I struck a wooden kitchen match and threw it into the hole.

Flames jumped up three feet high or more into the air as everything took fire. Back and forth and round and round the hole I paced, almost like a dance. I swayed in silence as the fire burned, almost like a circle dance or grass dance. I waited until everything was burnt to ashes, then I put the dirt back like I found it. It was like no hole had ever been there, as if nothing had been burnt there. It was as if nothing had ever happened.

Those fifteen years of foolishness and misery were gone. I felt my mind clear, experienced a sudden surge of lightness in my spirit. I was whole again, stronger, and able to press on with greater understanding.

The year was 1995 and I was fifty-three years old. After fifteen years of misery, I was finally free to move forward with my life.

Part Three

Full Circle

I started life infused by dreams
of childlike wonder—
bedazzled by the possibilities
until advancing years and their realities
set in and I began to drown in them.
Gone were the childish dreams,
along with endless hopes they carried with them.
I lost courage for awhile,
stopped seeing life as beautiful and wondrous,
forgot to look at daffodils and blue birds
and marvel at their symmetry,
lost track of what a blessed life I have.
But now my life has come full circle.
The wonder has returned
accompanied by hopes and possibilities
so great my mind can scarcely grasp them.

Chapter Eleven

Vision

A pastor told me once that when we "atone" we are "at one" with God. God accepted my atonement, and along with that acceptance He gave me clearer vision. I saw the entirety of my life with vision clarified by a deeper sense of love and understanding that welled up wanting to be shared somehow.

Figuratively, I hugged this new understanding of God and His purposes close to my heart. The world around me took on greater meaning. My eyes saw colors in brighter richer hues. Subtle sounds of nature moved me to rejoicing.

Something as simple as a rock worn smooth by water lay like diamonds in my hand while I gave thanks for finding such a treasure. With my reawakened spirit, life expanded into something other than the dreadful emptiness it had been for so long.

I'd read or heard accounts of people whose lives had been changed by God's grace, but I never took such reports to heart until John's message of the grass dance. Since then, my life has been transformed into a wondrous chronicle.

Prior to that period of darkness in the middle years of my life, I had always been spiritually introverted. I prayed and meditated in solitude, read and re-read every chapter of the Old Testament for the wisdom found there. God's amazing words recorded there seemed to make His plans for the world and everyone in it abundantly clear. That sense of childlike wonder left me for awhile when I was lost, but has since returned to me tenfold.

These days I read the Bible with a stronger sense of purpose and a greater curiosity. I am intrigued to realize that thousands of years ago God revealed to Old Testament prophets and common folk what scientists have only discovered to be true in the last couple hundred years. God gave His people light and water, air to breathe, food to eat, and beauty to surround them. He thought of everything, including loving, sharing, and nurturing to help us thrive as human beings. More than anything—I'm certain of it now—God intended us to love and be loved in abundance.

He wanted us to love the world He gave us and to be inspired by it. Speaking personally, it was my inability to grasp or accept the full measure of God's intentions that drew me from Him for a while. I became a doubter, accepting invisible air and atoms but rejecting an invisible God.

John's message of the grass dance erased my cynicism once and for all.

All my life I was a quiet person, prone to hiding my true thoughts except in prose or verse. More than anything, I feared rejection by God, man, everyone. I adored my husband, for example. On my part, it was a case of love at first sight, but it saddens me today to know he never fully realized that perhaps. I held that love safe in my heart where it could never be destroyed or wounded. I know now that God did not intend for us to horde and hide our love from the world. He meant for us to share it in the best way we know how.

From early childhood I was blessed with a good vocabulary and the ability to communicate in writing. I could always speak comfortably to large groups or converse with confidence one on one, as long as my heart and my emotions were not involved. I have never been able to speak aloud what I feel in the secret confines of my heart until recently.

While recording my experience with God and John and Grandpa, I thought a lot about my husband. He has always been a man with humor in his eyes and a mostly cheerful disposition. I was immediately drawn to the gentle joking way he had about him and his optimistic outlook. His life growing up in the mountains of Kentucky was far different from mine, which only made him all the more appealing to me. I loved the southern drawl he had, the way he looked at life with different opinions and expectations. My initial attraction to him quickly began to evolve into a love that has lasted more than 37 years.

My husband jokes a lot, but in reality he is a deep thinker.

He is a man of simpler and less complicated spirit than mine. He does not expect much from life or have delusions of grand accomplishments, as I am prone to do. He derives joy from the simple everyday things, such as our lasting marriage and our achievements as a couple. I have to hand it to him for his patience and for sticking with me through the good as well as hard times and all stages in between.

If rewards were handed out for long suffering or for persevering spouses, he would take the prize!

Ronald B. Johnson in 1965

My family and friends were skeptical about my marriage to a man I had not known all my life. They thought I should marry a local man, someone whose family's family they had known through several generations.

Even Grandma questioned my decision at first, until I lovingly reminded her how similar my situation was to hers when she and Grandpa wanted to get married.

I was blinded to any other prospect. I loved him. Those of lesser vision did not realize that what they perceived as his weak points became perfections in my eyes. It did not matter to me what they thought. I considered him God's blessing. I saw him clearly and looked at him with tunnel vision. Love can do that if we let it. I loved him as he was and is, and with the grace of God I always will. I believed in my youth that God put us together for a purpose, and I believe that more than ever now.

Does that seem corny? Maybe so. But I have learned that God provides for me in many loving ways and that includes the man He gave me for a husband.

Many years have come and gone since first I spied him standing by the water fountain in the Marysville city park.

He was laughing, joking with his friends. His happy face was open and free. Light brown hair was blowing in the Kansas summer wind. He was whipcord lean, tall, at ease with himself and life.

I sat in my friend Reita's '55 Ford convertible watching him in secret. It was a time of my life when love was the last thing on my mind. I surely was not looking for love, but it found me anyway. Just as my Grandma had when first she set her cap for Grandpa, I thought, "Here is a man I could love all my life." I wasn't wrong. So much has passed between us since that time, we have forgotten most of it. We've laughed and cried together over time, sharing life and creating bonds that nothing—no outside force of any kind—has been able to destroy.

When I was young, romantic love was new and frightening to me. I could scarcely see beyond tomorrow in those days and lived in breathless fear that love would end and he would go away. I love him still, but not with that youthful love so fearful he might leave and I would lose him.

These days, I love him with a calmness and a quiet heart, that knows we are together for a lifetime. My love for him is undiminished by time and wear. I thank my God for letting me see that clearly once again.

The wears and tears of life have changed us. Injuries, aging, and transient illnesses have sapped our strength compared to what it used to be. Such changes come to everyone who lives beyond a certain age. But buried deep inside our hearts and minds, love still lives unscathed and fresh.

I share these feelings with the world because the sharing serves a purpose. My husband is just one example of how God enhanced my vision of this life and every person, place, and thing in it. I share my feelings now because someone out there who has lost their way, given up on love or God or joy may be encouraged. Some reader may be seeing their world in shades of gray as I was for a while. I cannot promise that reclaiming joy and seeing the world in brighter colors will be easy. What I can promise, from personal experience, is that such happiness is possible. It's there within our reach and God will help us find the spirit of renewal and a clearer vision if we let Him.

Chapter Twelve

For Mother

Verla Mae Ford Smith

I cannot bring my story to a close without saying more about my mother. By now I have written in detail of the many wonderful and talented people who influenced my life from the day I was born. Grandma and Grandpa, aunts and uncles, all took an active role in raising me. They provided unwavering love, support, and encouragement in all that I set out to do, but the one who brought me into this world has given me the most. She laid the groundwork that would form the person I became.

In looking closely at the face and eyes reflected in her picture, I can see the joy and love that lived within her. Despite her many sorrows and disappointments, ill health and poverty, my mother's heart held joy. She loved the Lord and knew that He loved her and, in that knowing, Mom found a steady source of peace and joy. Everything about her demonstrated that, especially in the way she taught me by example as a child. When I made mistakes or misbehaved, she made an object lesson of that misstep. Mom held me close instead of pushing me away when I did wrong. Her corrections were made softly. She forgave and never once stopped loving, in the same true way God loves. Unconditionally. I didn't understand that fully until some time after John and Grandpa's revelation changed my life.

As I was prone to do with everyone I loved, I seldom said, "I love you," in spoken words to Mother. It wasn't because I was afraid or ashamed to speak of love out loud to Mom. It was just that "I love you" seemed like empty words to me compared to how I felt about her.

Countless times my mother gave whatever it took to help me realize my dreams. So many times, a dollar or two eked from her meager earnings made my way easier. Life wasn't easy for my mother. Life was not kind to her, but Mother's love for me was always clearly demonstrated. It was in her eyes, if not spoken outright. Mother's love for me was shown by everything she did, by sacrificing years and her youth to make life good for me. Hers was a legacy that never fully left me even when I lost my way and wandered for a while.

Even in those bad years when I was lost, people often saw a bit of Mom in me. I took it as the greatest compliment when people whispered, "She is so much like her mother!" I loved it when acquaintances of Mom's would go to her all smiles to brag on me a bit and make her beam with pride. She couldn't wait to tell me later what good things were said about me and who said them.

Mother's friendships were a joy and blessing to her also, just as mine are. Her friends often sought her out. They marveled at her loyalty and even disposition no matter what. They admired the way she "tilted at windmills" and her penchant for doing the right thing. When my friends compliment me, I silently give credit where credit is due.

I don't see myself in such a gracious light as they do.

Without my mother's influence I would have been a very different person. These days I smile in silence at such kind words aimed in my direction because I know the truth.

For the record now, I'd like to say it plainly for all the world to know. Thanks goes to Mom. I either learned or inherited my attitudes and behaviors from her. I got my soft nature and unworldliness from her. That kindness shining, from within me? My loyalty and undemanding ways?

All came from her.

All that's fine and true about me now, everything that speaks of love cannot be attributed to anything I do. It came from Mom and from the God who blessed me with her.

Thank God I gave Mom poems throughout her lifetime, saying everything that I've said here about her, and more. She had her tributes from me when she was alive to appreciate them.

I find it difficult, even now, to imagine mom and dad young and in love, dreaming hopeful dreams together. They were divorced when I was nine. Dad was married several more times and gone from our lives, until he came back home to spend the last few years of his life. One of the final lessons my mother taught me before she died was one of forgiveness. She said a little sternly to me one day when I had made some unkind comment about Dad, "Your father was a small town boy, an athlete. Oh how he loved to laugh and tell a funny joke! He loved to cook and had a quick, creative mind." Mom smiled sweetly as she said it, and her voice had a poignant sound to it as if she were remembering happy times. "Your father was a very different man before the army took him off to war in the Pacific. He came back to us broken. I've forgiven him for everything, and now you must forgive him too."

I didn't forgive him then. My heart was hard. But I have forgiven him now and I hope somewhere, somehow, my Mother knows that.

Chapter Thirteen

Working for the Wind

Clearer vision and improved understanding are a blessing, but can also be harsh taskmasters! Just when I thought my life was following the new path laid out for me, just as I began to make a few tentative plans, a mild sense of uncertainty began to nag at me. I sighed, I prayed to channel new- found creativity into wealth and fame and power.

But there remained lessons to be learned, human limitations to be faced. God's plan for me, it seems, varied quite a bit from mine.

All my life I had worked for money and all the trappings my wages could obtain. I worked for medical insurance and a pension plan. I don't mean to say that working is a bad thing. Society requires that we earn our own keep whenever we are able, expects us to pay our own way. I worked and took great pride in my ability to earn, relying on no one except my husband in the quest for financial security.

My husband and I worked hard for our money and were determined to enjoy it. We lived in diverse places and had decent houses that we remodeled every so often as the mood dictated. We drove new vehicles, the best we could afford. We had bass boats, new clothes, more shoes than we needed. We ate out frequently, spent money on other non-essentials because we could afford to, and watched our savings accumulate.

As a nurse I was passing fair. Working with people who needed my skills was a challenge. Not much caught me off guard. I reported to my shift on time and worked my scheduled hours reliably. Now and then I would go home filled with pride in a tough job well done. Just as often I would be disconsolate because of failed victories against human frailties, sorrows, death and disease. My bosses gave me glowing evaluations. I was proud of my abilities and the skills that had been learned over a lifetime in my profession.

Yes, I tried to do my best in all that I set out to do.

Sometimes I succeeded wonderfully and other times fell flat on my face, but I worked and kept on working to make a living. Except for that dark period when I turned away from God awhile, my whole life had been spent trying to "do the right thing." So where did this nagging little voice come from now that whispered, "You are working for the wind"?

"Working for the wind." That passage can be found in one of my favorite Old Testament books, *Ecclesiastes*, and it expresses perfectly what I did all my life. Those four words dug into my mind like a sharp rock rubbing in my shoe and would not go away.

"Working for the wind," can have many interpretations, I suppose. In my case it meant throwing good money after bad accumulating "things" just because I could. It meant laying up treasures on earth because that is expected of us, living a less than simple life so others could see how successful I was.

Working for the wind can be arrogance and foolish pride, an all-too-human frailty. As it did in my case, working for the wind can wreck health, blow minds, and come close to ruining lives. The longer I thought about that, the more it rankled. I had focused narrowly on working and having, getting and keeping, until the soul of me was dry and nearly dead. And here I was, still chasing riches and fame instead of basking in peace and contentment.

I believe in God and the gifts He grants each person, but that belief had always been disconnected from my work in the past. My work had always been right out front, laid on the line where all the world could see that I was a productive member of society. My gifts stayed hidden and unseen, part of a separate, secret life. I considered my work to be essential. God's gifts were simply extras to be indulged only when I had the energy or could spare the time.

Enhanced awareness since the dream has finally led to the conclusion that King Solomon was right when he described the futility of working for the wind. In my case at least, working only to accumulate money and things is not enough.

That bit of wisdom from Ecclesiastes remains as true today as it was in Solomon's time. To neglect God given gifts that bring me joy seems almost sinful somehow. Let me make it clear that these are my thoughts, my feelings as they relate to my own personal quest. This is not a judgment of or a recommendation to others. So how does a well past middle age woman like me stop working for the wind? How does she feed a desiccated spirit? And how does she identify and nourish long neglected gifts bestowed by God the day her spark of life began? Those were the questions I asked myself not so long ago.

This wasn't the first time I had searched for answers on my knees before God. It isn't the first time I found personal peace by heeding the answer to such prayers. It won't be the last. But this time, a calming presence touched me as I prayed and filled me with a clear resolve. I was reminded that the grass dance meant far more than dancing, more than grass. The grass dance was not meant to be my lesson in history or a story just for sharing. The grass dance was to be an icon, a reminder that my way of life had changed and God had been the One who changed it.

Succeeding or failing in my creative endeavors does not enter into my thinking these days. I revolve my world around God's wonders that come in many forms. The passage of my life has gone from happy and hopeful in the first few decades, to a period of darkness and despair, and finally to this current permanence of joy and peace. With God's guidance, I intend to soothe my spirit with His balm as long as I am able.

Chapter Fourteen

Morning Worship

One day in early summer, I returned to the cemetery where this odyssey began. My heart was full to bursting with anticipation of what further joys might await me. Prairie grass grown wild amongst the graves was hanging low with heavy dew. It was a perfect prairie morning, with just the slightest stirring of a fragrant breeze. All was quiet, except for bird songs sounding from the limbs of ancient trees, and the occasional call of meadowlarks from hiding.

I found what used to be John's grave. Its tiny marker was crumbled down to almost nothing from the weather, but I found the spot where John's bones rested. Growing scattered on and around his grave were sweet smelling, bright orange wildflowers. I can't put a name to the flowers growing wild there. The only other place I ever saw them was along the interstate in Illinois.

At nature's whim, the prairie wildflowers are scattered by the winds or birds and butterflies. One season they grow here, another there, but always in abundance. This season, nature in her unpredictability had chosen to decorate John's grave in wild profusion. I felt it was a special welcoming.

In ages past this graveyard had been open land. In John's younger days, before he was a hired man, this cemetery must have been a virgin prairie. How many praise songs had been sung to the Creator by John and his ancestors on this quiet hill?

How many ancient prayers were offered to Him here?

My imagination ran away with me that day, to other times and simpler ways, when John was young. I could see John's hardy prairie band the way they might have looked, some traveling afoot and others on the backs of loping ponies.

Prairie grass alive with scents of early morning might have brushed against John's legs as it did mine this day. He no doubt heard the sharp and warbling song of meadowlarks as they called out to each other. On the wind he might have heard the ripple of his family's laughter or the barking of a dog. All around him would have been the multicolored bob of wildflowers. Did he breathe in their sweetness then, just as I had now? Did John take into his heart and soul the sights and sounds of life around him and give thanks to his Creator for such gifts? All was silence for a time as I wondered what John's life was like more than a century ago when he was young, before this place became a graveyard.

Suddenly, I breathed a sigh and shuddered with the silent cry of joy that gripped me. As far as I could see was waving grass of greenish hues and wildflowers of every color. Above it all the morning sky was blinding radiant blue.

The air smelled fresh and pure. Nearby, a creek was gurgling across its bed of sand and stones. I could almost taste that cold sweet water on my tongue.

At that moment I left the modern world behind, however briefly. Life was pure and peaceful at that moment, as it was meant to be by our Creator. I felt no sense of future doom, no sorrow for the loss of pristine water, air or sky. I gave thanks for many gifts so richly given to this world by God. I softly sang a prayer of thanks and praise for all my blessings and raised my outstretched hands towards the sky as my heart-song strengthened. And I slowly swayed in ever-widening circles at John's grave. I didn't feel clumsy or foolish doing my imagined version of the grass dance. The time, the place, and God seemed to inspire this dancing worship. I felt like God was guiding me, in fact, towards some fitting culmination of the empty years I'd left behind me.

I worshiped God with all the energy within me, with my whole heart. I offered up my soul, with praise, and God accepted that gratuity. It was worship in the purest, most devoted form I'd ever known. It didn't cross my mind what someone might think if they should see me middle aged and overweight, dancing in a graveyard. I was not worried or embarrassed. I was thankful to have come full circle at last. Once again, I had become a part of God's continuum.

The present, past, and future of my life had finally come together at John's grave.

Chapter Fifteen

For John

I had come with hand-picked flowers for John's grave that day because I knew it would have pleased my grandma. Purple and yellow iris, deep rosey red and pinkish white peonies had been chosen carefully to make a cheery offering for John. I planned to lay the flowers at his head where once the gravestone stood, along with a letter written on a bit of sky blue paper I had purchased special for this day.

A long dark episode of my life began in this cemetery and it was fitting that it should end here. This ritual would signify officially the redirection of my life.

I sat cross-legged in the grass beside John's grave to write my letter to him. I felt clean inside, hopeful and free.

The words I wrote flowed easily, without my having to think about them. I thought about Grandma and Grandpa as I wrote, imagining their spirits hovering somewhere near me. Each word came straight from my heart to the old familiar friend the three of us had shared.

Dear John,

We never met face to face, but because of you, new life has been created and a child of God has been reborn.

I know from where you are this isn't as amazing as it seems to me. You've seen the mysteries of God first hand, but they are just a shadow to me here.

I want to thank you, John, for helping God reach out to me. Thank you for the years of friendship and devotion you invested in my grandparents. Thank you for loving God with simple purity and faith, without question.

I did a little grass dance for you, John, as best I could, around your grave. And I understand what you were saying, that a man's days are like the grass. I got the message.

Life is fleeting, so we ought to live it in the best way we know how.

And thanks to you I also know we go from life to death to life, just like the grass does, just like you and everyone there with you did.

I love you, John, in friendship like my Grandma and Grandpa did. How comforting it is to know the living circle you created with them did not end with death!

Thanks be to you and God, my friend!

Laurel

There were miracles that day amongst the graves. They weren't the sort of miracles you see reported in the press or on television specials. The world would not be clamoring at my door to make a movie of my miracles. But I felt God's hand upon my head in blessing as I sat beside John's grave that day.

I heard God whisper, "Peace," and felt His grace alive within me. Inside my mind I felt the soft explosion of assurance that a living Jesus had reached out to me in love. His mission to reclaim me was completed there that day beside John's earthly resting place. I folded up the letter and placed it underneath the flowers I had laid upon John's grave. That act was the beginning and the ending of a living circle once again complete. I remain within that same unbroken circle to this day. My husband, family and friends are with me there. So are Grandma, Grandpa, Mom, and John, along with all the loved ones who are with them in that blessed place beyond the grave that we call heaven. And at the center of our living circle was and is and always shall be our Creator, God.

What a blessed peaceful thing it is to know that.

This has been a the very personal story of an obscure life, an emotional quest, a fulfilling journey. Along the way I rediscovered faith and fed a starving spirit. My mission and my message are completed now, but I have some final thoughts to share with you before this story ends.

I have learned first hand that beyond the grave and in this life, there is no such thing as hopeless cases.

God helped me understand that nothing is too large or small for Him to manage. No person, place or thing has slipped beyond His grasp. He loves us all and wants us all to thrive.

I have learned that no sadness or defeat is final. The beauty God created is within us and around us, waiting for the opportunity to blossom and to bless us all with joy.

Mysteries the human mind can scarcely comprehend unfold

and come to life just beyond our vision. Messages of peace and hope reside in the world around us waiting to be seen and understood. The grass, flowers, and trees wither and fade, only to return again in season. And so it is with everything in life.

God speaks. All we have to do is listen. God forgives. All we have to do is believe it. God renews even the tired and cynical spirit. All we have to do is accept it. That was and is the true message of the grass dance. God has become far more to me than some impersonal deity reigning in the heavens out of sight. My God is John's One-True-Creator-Spirit. I know this God. I see and feel His presence. He is tangible and real, the way He was for John. Saying that, my story ends.

From safe within the living and unbroken circle of God's love, I wish you peace.

Printed in the United States
104477LV00003B/171/A

9 781588 514455